GW00372264

# Fitness for the Over-50s

A guide to healthy living
with gentle exercise for the not so young,
into and on after retirement.

## Barbara Roberton

**Patrick Stephens**
**Wellingborough, Northamptonshire**

My grateful thanks to
Pamela, Daphne and Patrick

First published in 1988


British Library Cataloguing in Publication Data

Roberton, Barbara
   Fitness for the over fifties.
   1. Physical fitness for the middle aged.
   2. Physical fitness for the aged
   I. Title
   613.7      RA777.5

   ISBN 1-85260-050-0

*Patrick Stephens Limited is part of
the Thorsons Publishing Group,
Wellingborough, Northants,
NN8 2RQ England*

Printed in Great Britain by
Woolnough Bookbinding,
Irthlingborough,
Northants

10   9   8   7   6   5   4   3   2   1

# CONTENTS

# INTRODUCTION

This is a fitness book with a difference — it is specially designed for the over 50s, so that by the time retirement comes you are fit and healthy and ready to enjoy the extra time you have earned.

Retirement is a time for relaxation without the stresses and strains of work — but it is a mistake to 'take it easy' with your body. There is no reason why you can't be even fitter after retirement than you were before you retired.

There is no need to follow a hard regime of exercise, but a programme of regular, gentle exercise will not only keep you feeling fit and healthy but also happy and active whatever your age.

## How to start

Take a look around you at all the elderly people you know and decide — do you want to be like Mr and Mrs A, who are constantly busy and always seem happy and have time to do everything that is going on? Or do you want to be like Mr and Mrs X, who sit about all day complaining about their aches and pains and how cold it is? Easy choice, really, isn't it? So let's get started.

## What kind of exercise

There are many ways of keeping fit and healthy, and you can choose the ones you enjoy most.

Walking, swimming and cycling are ideal, all round forms of exercise. You may enjoy gardening, ballroom dancing or joining an exercise class. The exercises in this book are muscle toning exercises based on my many years experience as a teacher of ballet, tap and keep fit. They are aimed at toning your muscles, keeping your joints loose and free from stiffness and generally helping you to feel as good in your sixties as you did in your forties.

## Benefits of exercise

People who remain fit and healthy in their later years almost certainly do so because they have maintained a high level of physical activity. But it is never too late to start — you are never too old to be fit. With just a little willpower and, of course, a sensible diet you can maintain:

- a firm tummy
- an upright posture
- loose joints
- increased stamina and vitality
- a feeling of being generally healthier and happier

## Think fit

Attitude is the key — if you *think* fit and healthy *you will be* fit and healthy. Use the extra time you have to create a positive attitude towards your lifestyle, your health and well being. Enjoy being fit and healthy — you will be amazed at the difference it makes in your life. It is also infectious — your friends and family will notice the new, fit, happy you.

## Time to exercise

Get into the habit of exercising. Make it part of your

routine, like eating and sleeping. YOU OWE IT TO YOUR BODY to say young and fit whatever your age. You spend all your life growing old — spend some time each day on staying active and healthy in body and mind. Use everyday tasks as a form of exercise. Always exercise with care, however; if you are starting on a fitness programme in your later years the important thing is to start slowly and gently and work up gradually to a level of exercise you are happy with.

## Diet

As you grow older there is no need to change your eating habits, as long as you continue to eat a sensible diet. However, as people grow older they tend to put on weight due to the fact that they are less active. So the obvious remedy is not to allow yourself to become less physically active than you were. Eat a sensible, mixed diet and a little less of it.

Foods that are very rich in fat are ones to be avoided, so do cut down on butter, cream and cheese (except cottage cheese), fat meats and processed meats.

Do eat plenty of fresh vegetables and fruit. Cut down on your intake of alcohol and please, if you still smoke, STOP! Smoking probably presents the most serious risk to health for not only does it have an effect on the heart and blood vessels, making it a major contributor to heart attacks and strokes, but it also damages the lungs. So stop smoking now and reap the benefits.

## Stress — and relaxation

During the working life we are subjected to an

assortment of problems that cause feelings of tension and stress. Stress is responsible for all sorts of symptoms, — aches and pains, headaches, and at worst angina and heart attacks. With retirement those stresses and tensions should lessen — but even so it is very important to relax. The art of relaxation has to be learned and practised. Give yourself a few moments every day to unwind and slow down.

Always relax after exercising — use the time to slow down your heart and pulse rate. Let the worked muscles cool slowly and so prevent cramps and strains.

## What to wear

Be comfortable — never exercise in tight clothing, be unrestricted and warm. Muscles need to be kept warm in order to prevent injury. Shoes, if worn, should be well fitting and secure. Always remove any jewellery that might get caught and cause an accident.

After exercising wrap up well and cool down slowly by relaxing as explained at the end of the exercise section and you need never feel stiff, catch a chill or strain anything.

## Pain

IF IT HURTS — STOP! There are two kinds of pain. There is a stiffness that we get when we exercise vigorously after doing very little for a long time. This means your body is working hard — it is only temporary — take a hot bath and it will soon pass. Then there is injury pain that is sharp and stabbing — this should be investigated. Don't make unreasonable demands on your body — start slowly and build up to a level that you can maintain. Listen to your body and if it tells you to stop — stop.

## Before exercising

Always make sure you have an empty bladder. Don't eat a heavy meal or drink alcohol. This could result in cramp and nausea. Relax and prepare to enjoy your work-out routines.

## Check list

If you have any heart condition, hypertension or serious varicose veins you should consult your doctor as to the level of exercise he considers sensible for you.

Remember the golden rule: IF IT HURTS — STOP!

Pay special attention to all exercises involving the back. NEVER STRAIN. Start very slowly and proceed gently.

Exercising should be fun as well as beneficial. So make sure you enjoy the movements. Exercise with your partner or a friend and keep fit together.

## How to use this book

To do all the exercises in part one of this book will take one hour. This is your goal but DO NOT TRY TO DO ALL THE EXERCISES THE FIRST TIME. Start slowly and work your way up. Use the book to suit your needs and daily routine. Don't try too much too soon. At the first attempt, exercise for about ten minutes (including warming up). At the next session work for about fifteen minutes and so on, building up the number of repetitions and the length of time you exercise for. Listen to your body — it will soon tell you when you have done enough. You will soon reach the ideal.

You will see a box at the top of each page. This gives you the ideal number of repeats to aim for.

The second part of the book deals with exercises for those with special problems, those who are not as mobile as they used to be. It includes exercises to do sitting in a chair and also lying in bed.

So whatever age you are you can reap the benefits of exercise. You owe it to your body to get fit and keep fit.

People today live longer than ever before and, in general, their quality of life is better. With the help of this book the aim is to have many happy years of fit and healthy retirement.

# WARM UP

Before exercising it is essential that your muscles are well warmed up in order to prevent strains and pulls.

| Warm Up | 5 Mins. |
| --- | --- |

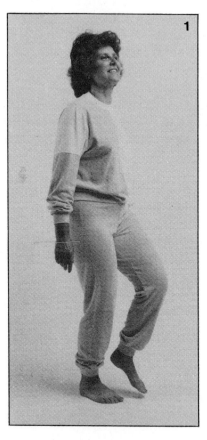

Stand up tall, tummy and bottom pulled in and start by walking (1). Continue walking and at the same time stretch your arms up above your head in a circular motion (2).

10

Lift your knees up, one at a time and feel the thighs and hips loosen (3). Gradually work into a trot (4). Do this on the spot and keep going for about two minutes. Breathe in through your nose and out through your mouth. Then gently bounce on the spot (5).

You should now be feeling warm, your heart beating steadily and eager for more.

# LOOSEN UP

Get rid of stiffness in your back and legs by toe touching. Stand with your feet apart, take the right hand over to your left foot (6) and straighten up (7). Then take your left hand over to your right foot (8) and straighten up. Place both hands on the floor between your feet (9), push forwards three times and then straighten up.

Don't worry if you can't reach your toes, you can bend your knees a little to begin with. This soon won't be necessary.

| Toe touches | 10 |
| 2 Hands over | 10 |
| Fold in half | 10 |

Next take both hands over to your left foot (10), straighten up and then take both hands to your right foot.

Now place both feet together, stand up straight — then fold in half (11).

# WAIST TRIMMER

| Waist trimmer | 8 |
| Arm outstretched | 8 |
| Hands on hips | 8 |
| Hands behind head | 8 |

Keep your back straight, feet apart and bend sideways from the waist, pushing your arm down your leg towards your ankle (12). Do four pushes to the right, four to the left and then eight pushes from side to side.

Try the same exercise with your arm outstretched (13), four to each side and then eight from side to side.

Then place your hands on your hips and push from the waist (14). Next, try this exercise with your hands behind your head (15).

# WAIST STRETCH

| Waist stretch | 10 |
| Holding hip | 10 |
| Palm up | 10 |

Stand with your feet apart and push from the waist taking your left arm over your head (16). Push four times. Then take the right arm over and push to the left four times (17).

Try the same exercise holding your hip with the opposite hand (18). Do four pushes to each side.

Release your hip and take your right hand over your head and push from the waist, this time with the palm of your hand facing the ceiling (19).

# THIGHS

Jump and lift your knee as high as you can (20). One leg

| Knees up | 50 |
| --- | --- |
| X jumps | 30 |

then the other. Swing your arms freely and keep going for as long as you feel comfortable.

*Don't over do things* — start carefully and build up gradually. *IF IT HURTS — STOP.*

Next jump your feet apart and jump them back together again. Do four jumps with your arms by your side (21) and then four jumps taking your arms up to form an 'X' (22).

Breathe in through your nose and out through your mouth. This will stop you panting. Should you feel any discomfort in the chest — stop and rest.

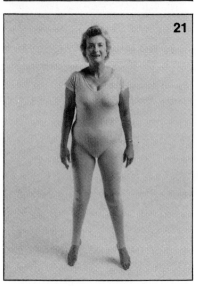

# ARM SWINGS

| Arm swings | 12 |
|---|---|
| Men's arm flings | 10 |
| Ladies' bust toner | 20 |
| Gripping wrists | 20 |

Stand with your feet apart. Swing your right arm backwards three times (23), then the left arm (24). Swing both arms in front of your face (25) three times in one direction and then three times in the other direction.

# CHEST FLINGS — FOR MEN

Bring your arms in to cross your chest (26). Fling your arms back (27) then in again. This will strengthen your back and upper arm. Start with just three or four and work towards the ideal.

# BUST TONER — FOR LADIES

Stand with feet apart. Place your fingers on your shoulders (28) and draw circles in the air with your elbows in a backwards direction.

Next grip your wrists and hold them at shoulder height. Force your hands to slide up your arms towards your elbows (29).

You can also do this exercise in a sitting position.

# FLOOR WORK

Always use a mat or a towel for floor work — not only does this cushion your back, it also stops you sliding about, especially if you are on a polished floor.

Lie flat for a few seconds. Relax and let go!

Try to tighten each of your muscles separately. Work your way through your calves, thighs and tummy. Then tighten your bottom. Let everything go.

Remember, don't strain. Do all the exercises at your own pace — build up gradually.

All 'sit ups' should be done through a curved spine and don't forget the golden rule, *IF IT HURTS — STOP.*

# TUMMY TONER

Lie flat, hands by your sides touching your legs. Slowly raise your head and shoulders,

| | |
|---|---|
| Half sit | 10 |
| Triangle | 10 |

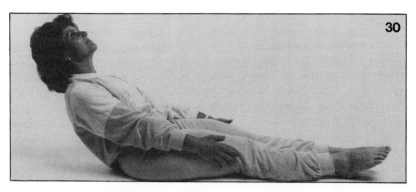

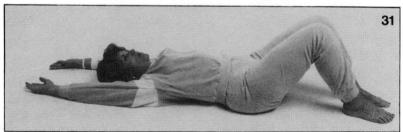

allowing your hands to slide along your thighs towards your knees (30). You should be at a 45° angle. Do not sit right up. Let yourself down again gently.

Lie flat, knees up, with your feet flat on the floor, close to your bottom: stretch your arms above your head (31). Pull up, swinging your arms over your head to touch your toes and thus form a triangle (32). Allow your heels to lift

slightly, then relax and return to the floor.

# SIT UPS AND STRETCHES

| | |
|---|---|
| Sit ups | 10 |
| Hands on hips | 10 |
| Hands behind head | 10 |

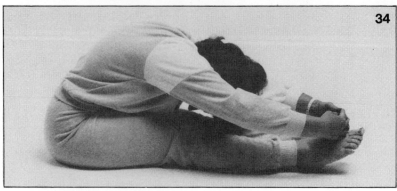

Lie flat, then sit up and reach up with your arms (33). Feel your diaphragm lift and pull your tummy in — fold in half (34). Lie back down again.

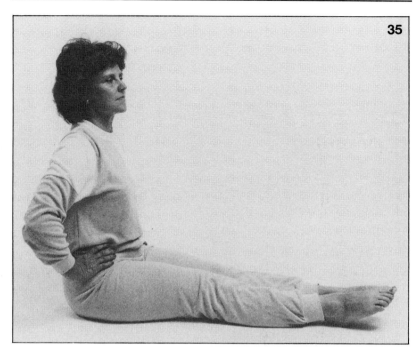

Now try sitting up with your hands on your hips (35).

Next place your hands behind your head and sit up (36).

If you find this hard to do, try anchoring your feet. Hook them under the bed, or ask someone to hold them for you.

25

# TUMMY AND THIGH TONER

| Leg lifts | 6 sets |
| Leg cross overs | 10 |

Lie flat, support your lower back with your hands. Lift one leg at a time quite slowly (37). Now lift both legs together (38). Lower them slowly but don't touch the floor — lift them both up again: then lower them to the floor. Make your tummy do the work, control the legs — don't let them crash to the ground.

Lie flat. Lift both legs up and take them as wide apart as you can (39). Bring them together and let them cross over (40). Continue crossing and opening for as long as is comfortable.

Lie flat and relax for a few seconds.

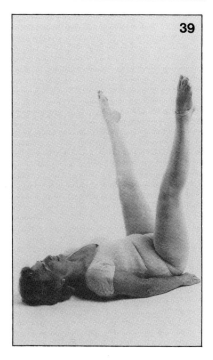

# LEGS

Lie flat and cushion your back with your hands. Lift your legs up and cycle in the air (41). Keep going for as long as you can.

| | |
|---|---|
| Cycling | 50 |
| Hands behind head | 20 |
| Leaning on elbows | 20 |
| Sitting cycles | 20 |

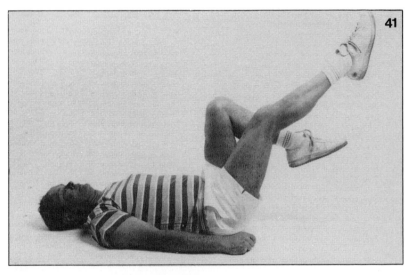

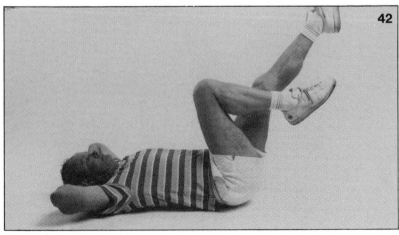

Next place your hands under your head and continue cycling (42).

Lean back on your elbows and cycle (43).

Then sit up and cycle on the floor (44).

Have a rest: wriggle your legs to release any tension in the thighs or hips.

**43**

**44**

# HIPS AND BOTTOM

| | |
|---|---|
| Hip roll | 50 |
| Bounce | 50 |
| Walks | 20 each way |

This couldn't be easier. Simply roll on your hips and bottom, distributing your weight over the offending parts! (45). It's so easy, you can roll for ages.

Now bounce on your bottom and pound away any unwanted inches (46).

Walk forward on your bottom (47) and then walk back again. You can walk around for as long as you like.

47

# FOR A SUPPLE BACK

Roll over onto your tummy and lie flat. Very gently push up with your hands from the waist (48). Keep your shoulders down and your elbows tucked in. *Don't strain — if it hurts — stop.*

| | |
|---|---:|
| Push up | 5 |
| Leg lift | 5 on |
| | each leg |
| Legs together | 5 |

Lie flat and lift one leg up at a

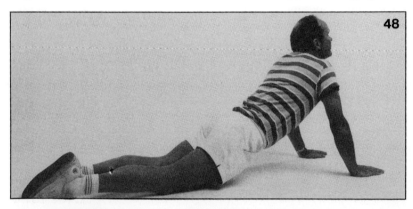

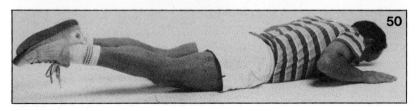

time (49). Lift them very gently. Then lift both legs together (50). Relax and rest for a moment and then repeat the whole exercise.

Now lie flat. Push up onto your knees (51) and push on back into a tucked position (52), keeping your arms well out in front of you. Then push forward (53) and back down to the floor.

# LEG STRETCHES

Sit up with your back straight, tummy pulled in and feet wide apart (54). Take your right hand over to your left foot (55), then your left hand over to your right foot (56). Then fold in half and reach for your toes, pushing forward three times (57).

When you feel comfortable doing this try sitting with your feet together and fold in half (58).

# HIPS AND UPPER THIGHS

| | |
|---|---:|
| Leg lifts | 40 |
| Knee lifts | 10–20 on each side |

**59**

**60**

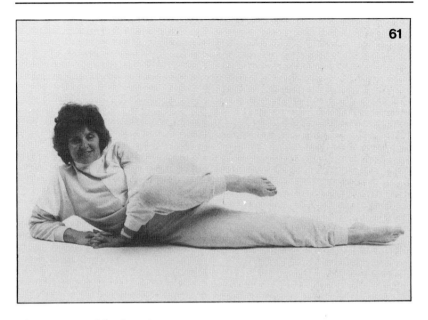

Lie on your side, keeping your hips well forward (59). Throw your leg up (60) and keep going for as long as you can.

Then bend your knee and bring it up towards your face (61). Start with ten on one side and then turn over and do ten on the other side.

# TOP TO TOE STRETCH

| | |
|---|---|
| Pull ups | 20 |
| Swings | 12 |
| Climbs | 20 |

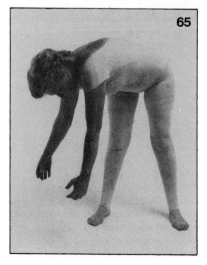

Pull up onto your toes (62) and feel yourself stretch as you reach up with your hands. Bend your knees and crouch down into a tucked position (63). Continue up and down.

Swing your arms and body in a circular motion from the waist, letting your hands touch the floor as you go round (64, 65, 66, 67). Swing round in one direction and then the other.

Now try climbing up an imaginary rope (68), really stretching as you reach up.

# LEG SWINGS AND LUNGES

**69**

| Leg swings | 25 |
| Knee turns | 25 |
| Lunges | 10 on |
| | each leg |

Stand up straight. Swing your leg forward from the hip, up as high as you can, ideally to 90° (69), let it swing back and up behind you as high as it will go (70). Keep swinging the legs alternately until they tire.

**70**

Now lift your knee in front of you (71) and turn it out to the side (72). Do this alternately for as long as you can.

Stand up straight with outstretched arms (73), lunge forward with your right foot (74) and then step back, feet together again. Make ten lunges on your right foot and then ten lunges on the left foot.

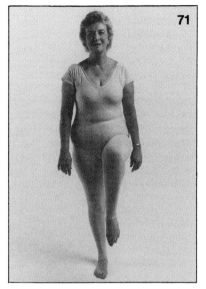

# WAIST TURNS

| | |
|---|---|
| Waist turns | 50 |
| Double push | 30 |
| Hands on hips | 50 |

Stand up straight with feet apart and arms shoulder high at a 90° angle to your body (75). Make sure that you keep your hips and knees perfectly still and turn from the waist (76). Try to do at least twenty turns, always ensuring that only your top half is moving.

Next try a double push to each side.

Now place your hands on your hips and turn from the waist (77). Be sure to keep your hips and knees still.

Then have a flop and a rest (78).

# TUMMY TONER

Sit on the edge of a sturdy upright chair. Keep your back straight and hold onto the edge (79). Draw your knees up (80). Extend your legs and hold for five counts, keeping your tummy pulled in tight (81). You will feel your tummy pull, so only do two extentions to begin with. If your back hurts — don't do it.

# THIGH TIGHTENER

Sit upright on the chair (82). Touch your left toe with your right hand (83), and then your right toe with your left hand. Keep touching the opposite toe for as long as you can. Keep your back straight and don't slouch.

Now lean back on the chair, lift your legs off the ground and cycle (84). Keep going for as long as is comfortable. Don't forget the golden rule: IF IT HURTS — STOP.

# COOL DOWN

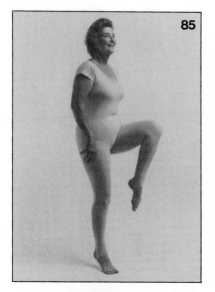

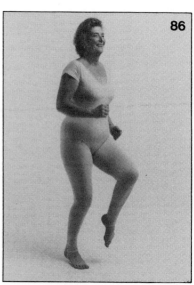

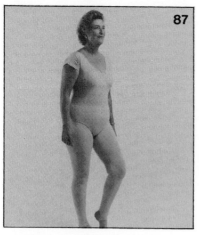

tension in the worked muscles.

Cooling down is just as important as warming up. It allows the heart and pulse to slow down gradually and naturally. It also releases any Skip (85) or jog (86) on the spot for about two minutes. Then walk, keeping your shoulders back and your tummy pulled in (87). Feel yourself slow down gradually until you finally flop (88).

# RELAXATION

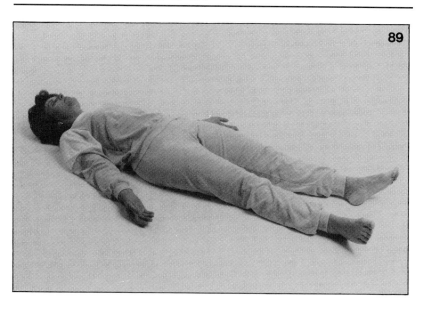

Relaxation is so important. After any exercise you must give your body time to slow down and cool down.

Put on a warm sweater or track suit, switch on some peaceful music and lie down (89). A lovely piece of music is *Gymnopédie 1* and *3* by Erik Satie.

Make yourself comfortable and feel any tightness release.

Start by relaxing your toes and work your way throughout the whole of your body.

Breathe in through your nose and out through your mouth. Close your eyes and 'float'. Stay there for about five minutes or until the music stops. Then have a wriggle and sit up when you are ready. You will feel wonderful. Calm and rested and ready to tackle anything.

# SPECIAL PROBLEMS

So far in this book we have dealt with people who are generally fit and healthy. There are, of course, others who are less fortunate and their level of exercise has to be determined by the severity of their problem.

An *asthmatic*, for example, may not be able to run on the spot for more than a few steps — but sit ups may present no difficulty at all. Each individual can find a level of exercise and follow a routine of healthy living.

*Diabetics* and those with *hypertension* are encouraged to exercise, but you should consult your doctor if you are starting to exercise for the first time.

It is common in hospitals to provide supervised exercise for *heart attack* patients and results have proved tremendously beneficial to the patient. But don't exercise if you have had a recent heart attack without first consulting your doctor.

Aches and pains associated with *rheumatism* and *arthritis* are generally accepted as part of growing old — yet if you keep yourself supple and active there is no need to suffer the pain of stiff joints. It is essential to keep muscles and joints moving, just as it is to keep an engine well lubricated. All arthritis and rheumatism can be helped with gentle exercise.

*Varicose veins* are more often seen amongst women than men. Good circulation is the best defence against varicose veins and regular exercise will stimulate the circulation.

*A regular exercise programme will not only keep your muscles in tune and condition your heart and lungs, but it will also ensure that your body does not grow old too quickly.*

*You can control a lot of the ageing of your body and it is a mistake to think that age is a signal to slow down physically.*

# WARMING UP IN A CHAIR OR IN BED

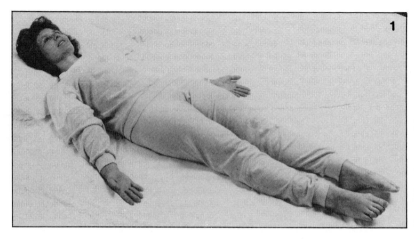

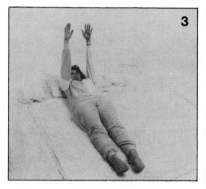

You can warm up anywhere — in a chair or even in bed. Before attempting any exercise you must ensure that you are warm and that your muscles are warmed up. This is important to prevent strains and pulls. If you are not very mobile it is perfectly all right to warm up lying on a bed.

Lying on the bed have a slow

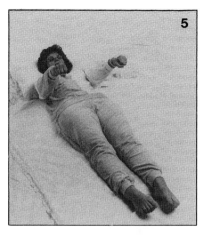

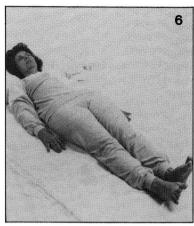

general stretch (1). Lift up your right arm (2) and then your left arm (3). Push both arms forward at the same time, opening your fingers wide (4). Pull back your arms slowly, closing your hands (5). Repeat this two or three times.

Next wriggle your toes (6). Turn your ankles — clockwise five times and then anti-clockwise five times. Then wave your feet, up and down.

Draw your right knee up (7): put it down. Then draw your left knee up — and down. Then draw both knees up (8) and put them down. Repeat this three or four times then relax.

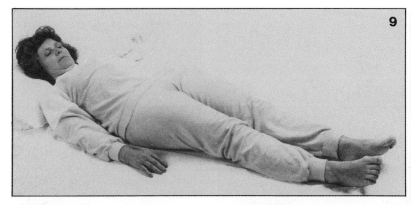

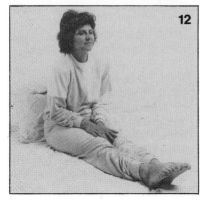

Flex your tummy muscles (9).

Flex your buttocks — then relax.

Sit up and shrug your shoulders (10).

Push your shoulders back (11) and roll your shoulders forward (12) — push the shoulders forward and back five times.

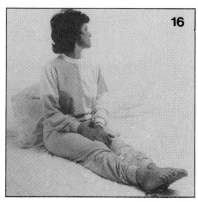

Drop your head forward onto your chest (13) and then gently push your head back (14). Push forward and back gently three times.

Turn your head to your right shoulder (15) and then to your left (16). Roll from side to side three times. Next roll your head round in a circle (17) three times more in one direction and then three times in the other.

# GET UP

If you can stand on your feet, even for a short period continue your warm up with this exercise.

Stand up straight and take a couple of deep breaths — in through your nose and out through your mouth.

Lift up your right knee to thigh height (18) and place feet back together again. Lift the right knee five times and then lift the left knee five times. Walk on the spot (19) and, if you are able, work up to a gentle trot on the spot (20).

You will now be feeling warm and loose — if you are mobile you can choose any exercises from the first part of the book — but do be sensible and be aware of your limitations. If you are not able to do any of the exercises from the first part of the book the following exercises may help you. Always remember, IF IT HURTS — STOP.

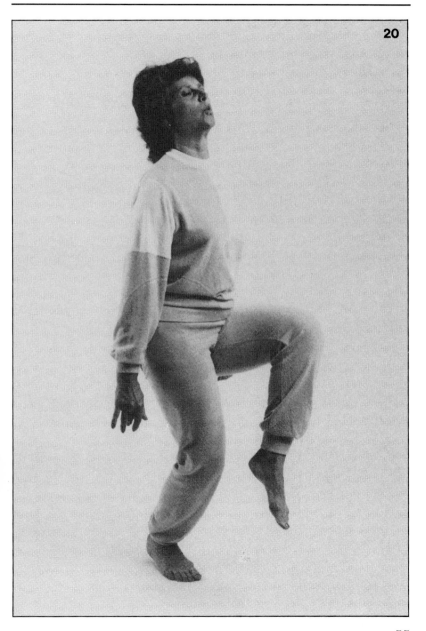

# EXERCISES TO INCREASE HIP MOTION

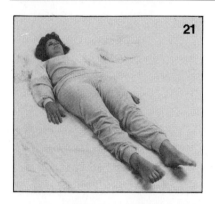

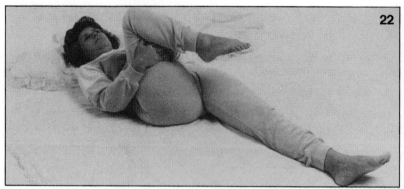

Lie flat (21). Draw your right knee up towards your chest — hold your leg under the knee (22). Then draw up your other knee.

Next lie flat — bend up both knees keeping your feet flat (23). Hug your knee — pointing your foot towards your bottom (24), first one leg then the other.

Now lie flat with both knees bent — feet flat. Drop your right knee to the floor or the bed (25) and return the knees together. Drop your left knee to the floor. Then bring your knees together.

If any of these exercises pull on your back — stop.

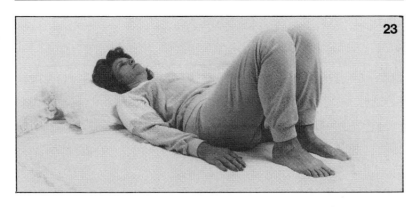

# EXERCISES SITTING IN A CHAIR

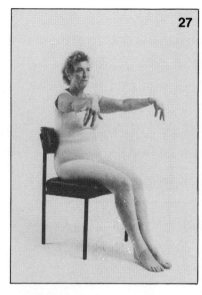

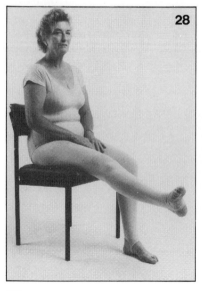

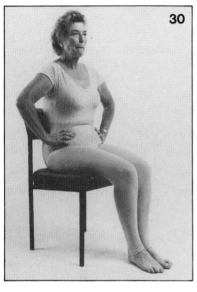

To loosen your shoulders and upper torso, reach high above your head with your hands clasped (26). Stretch and then relax five times.

For increased mobility of your wrists and ankles, rotate your wrist — first one way and then the other (27).

Rotate your ankles — first one way and then the other (28)

Now rotate wrists and ankles together — first in one direction and then in the other (29).

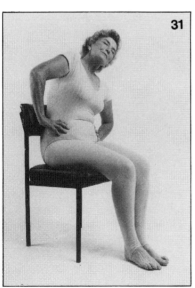

To loosen your waist, put your hands on your hips (30) and push from the waist to your right, four times (31) and then push four times to the left.

# LEG STRENGTHENERS

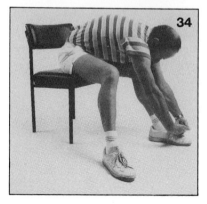

Sit upright. Touch your right foot with your left hand (32). Then take your right hand to your left foot (33).

Sit upright. Bend over your left foot (34). Sit up.

Then bend over your right foot (35). Keep your tummy pulled in.

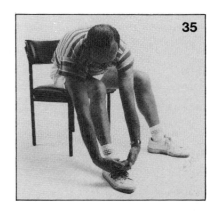

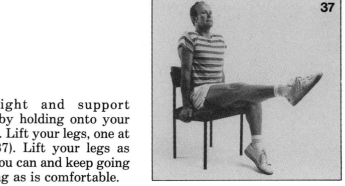

Sit upright and support yourself by holding onto your chair (36). Lift your legs, one at a time (37). Lift your legs as high as you can and keep going for as long as is comfortable.

# SELF MASSAGE

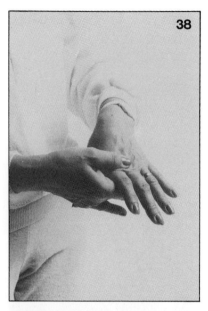

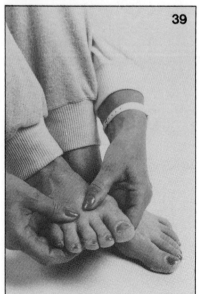

Massaging your own hands, fingers (38) and feet (39) can be most beneficial. Gentle stretching of the fingers and toes can help to loosen stiff joints.

Always remember the golden rule — IF IT HURTS — STOP.

You are never too old to exercise and it is never too late to start. Start very gently and work up gradually.

Enjoy your latter years — be fit and healthy and you will find your retirement most rewarding.

Think fit and healthy — be fit and healthy.

A wonderful exercise for your face is to *smile* (40).

**Other recommended reading...**
*(Also by Barbara Roberton)*

# FAMILY FITNESS

The message that exercise is the key to a happy and healthy life is getting through to more and more people—and not just individuals. Whole families are discovering the benefits of regular exercise together. This bright friendly book is designed to encourage and not to cajole and is packed with ideas and exercise routines to get your family fitter.

# FITNESS AND FUN FOR CHILDREN

This book is for youngsters of all ages—from the very small to the nearly grown-up. It doesn't matter how young or old you are, anyone can have lots of fun with exercise.

The fun-filled exercises in this book will stimulate children to:

● learn the benefits of excerise
● have fun with practical, enjoyable fitness routines
● develop a healthy enthusiasm for staying fit.